ENDORSEMENTS

An excellent book for aircrew members. The techniques are simple yet effective and employ all of the principles taught in self-defense and control tactics.

DICK WEBER, *retired 28-year veteran of the FBI, Defensive Tactics Instructor (1972–'98), Program Manager for Defensive Tactics at the FBI Academy (1981–'87), Defensive Tactics Instructor for the FBI Hostage Rescue Team (1987–'89).*

I find it to be the most concise, complete and easy to understand self-defense course of its type I have ever seen. This may be the breakthrough course for aircrew and flight attendants. Congratulations on developing a simple to understand and easy to perform course of self-defense instruction.

PHILIP KING, *former US Naval Special Warfare Officer and FBI Special Agent*

NEVER AGAIN

Rich & Geselle —

Don't try any of this "stuff" at home!
Fly safe
God bless

NEVER AGAIN

A Self-Defense Guide for the Flying Public

Mark H. Bogosian
Tommy L. Hamilton
Michael K. Regan

Brown Books Publishing Group
Dallas, Texas

Never Again
© 2004 Crew Defense Tactics, LLC

All rights reserved. No part of this publication may be reproduced, stored in any retrieval system, or transmitted in any form or by any means, mechanical, photocopying, recording, or otherwise, without prior written permission from the authors and Crew Defense Tactics, LLC

Manufactured in the United States of America.

For information, please contact:
Brown Books Publishing Group
16200 North Dallas Parkway, Suite 170
Dallas, Texas 75248
www.brownbooks.com
972-381-0009
or
Crew Defense Tactics
310 S. Park Blvd. #315
Grapevine, TX 76051
CrwDefTactics@aol.com

ISBN 0-9744597-2-0
LCCN 2004100063
2 3 4 5 6 7 8 9 10

ACKNOWLEDGMENTS

This book would not have been possible without the support and encouragement of our families and friends.

Special thanks to Jana Bogosian for playing such an important role in the book's production.

Thanks also to Don Beste for lending us his expertise. And Jeff Crilley, your input was key!

We would also like to thank Milli Brown, Deepa Pillai, Alyson Alexander, Cathy Williams, Kathryn Grant, and Erica Jennings at Brown Books for the urgency, professionalism, and great care they lent to this project.

DEDICATION

This book is dedicated to those who lost their lives in the tragic events of September 11, 2001.

ABOUT THE AUTHORS

MARK H. BOGOSIAN

Mark Bogosian is a 1983 graduate of the United States Air Force Academy. He was a C-130 aircraft commander at Pope Air Force Base, North Carolina, where his special qualifications included SOLL II (Special Operations Low Level II). He was also a C-21 Lear Jet aircraft commander and instructor pilot at Barksdale Air Force Base, Louisiana. Mark has flown as a first officer on the Boeing MD-80 and as a captain on the Fokker F-100. He is currently a first officer on the Boeing 757/767 for a major U.S. airline.

TOMMY L. HAMILTON

Tommy Hamilton is a police lieutenant with the Dallas/Fort Worth International Airport Department of Public Safety. He has spent the past thirteen years with the Special Weapons and Tactics (SWAT) Team and has served on the Entry Team, the Sniper Team, and worked as an FBI-trained hostage negotiator. Lt. Hamilton has served as the team leader/sergeant and is currently the SWAT Team Commander, with a specialty in Tactical Training. He is qualified to teach Special Weapons and Tactics, both basic and advanced levels, and has also taught courses in chemical weapons, bus and vehicle assaults, aircraft assaults, and building assaults. His specialties have included narcotic raids and riot control. Lt. Hamilton has trained with the military Special Forces in the United States and in Israel, Germany, and Argentina.

Lt. Hamilton also teaches at several police academies and community colleges in the Dallas/Fort Worth area, where he is a staff instructor in Defensive Tactics. Courses taught include self-defense, weapon retention, defensive knife, police baton, pressure point control tactics, ground fighting, joint locks and manipulation, takedowns, handcuffing, and kicks and strikes. He is a four-time recipient of the Nick Fowler Top Instructor Award at the Tarrant County College Basic Police Officer's Academy and has received the Top Instructor Award at the Cedar Valley College Police Academy. He is also a First Degree Black Belt with the Korean Yudo Association. Lt. Hamilton has been called as an expert witness in police use of force and was recently asked to teach aircraft assaults to foreign military and civilian specialized units for the State Department. He is the past regional director of the Texas Tactical Police Officer's Association and teaches courses in Critical Incident Response for the Federal Law Enforcement Training Center in Glynco, Georgia. He also teaches classes on violence in the workplace.

Michael K. Regan

Michael Regan has been employed by the North Central Texas Council of Governments for the past nine years, and is currently serving as manager of the Regional Training Center. He was the senior police training coordinator prior to occupying his current position. He also teaches courses in personal protection, violence in the workplace, and women's safety issues. He is an active Texas Peace Officer and is also a United States Air Force veteran with over twenty-nine years of service. While in the military, he completed his bachelor's degree in business at the University of Maryland and several master's level courses in public administration. Mike has also completed over six hundred hours of specialized training in ground combat defense. He is currently completing a master's degree in education from Saint Joseph's University and is a graduate of the Air Force Command Ground Combat Defense School and the FBI Anti-Terrorism Course.

DISCLAIMER

The authors and Crew Defense Tactics, LLC do not assume responsibility for the use or misuse of the various procedures and techniques contained in this book. Crew Defense Tactics, LLC and the authors have taken reasonable precautions in the preparation of this book and specifically disclaim any liability resulting from the use or application of the information contained herein. Training sessions using the various procedures and techniques contained herein should be conducted under the supervision of a qualified self-defense instructor.

WARNING: If you are under the care of a physician, if you are presently taking any prescribed medication, or if you have any pre-existing health problems, consult with a medical professional first before practicing any of the following maneuvers or techniques on your own or participating in any training sessions involving this book.

This book can be adapted and specifically tailored to fit all modes of public transportation.

TABLE OF CONTENTS

	Introduction	xv
1.	A Word to Passengers	1
2.	Terrorist Psychological Profile	3
3.	Identifying a Potential Problem/Terroristic Threat	9
4.	Passenger Reactions	13
5.	Crisis Management	17
6.	Use of Force Factors	19
7.	Levels of Force Continuum	21
	I. Professional Presence	22
	II. Verbal Communications	23
	III. Physical Contact	27
8.	Concepts of Close Quarter Tactics	29
9.	Target Areas of the Human Body	31
10.	Close Quarter Maneuvers and Tactics	35
	I. Weapons of the Body	36
	II. Stances	46
	III. Strikes	48
	IV. Blocks	56
	V. Ground Fighting Techniques	60
	VI. Kicks/Knee Strikes	75

11.	Weapon Takeaways	137
	I. Gun Takeaways	139
	II. Knife/Box Cutter Takeaways	150
12.	Combination Maneuvers	165
13.	The Use of Commonly Found Objects on an Aircraft	173
	I. Cockpit Items	174
	II. Flight Attendant Carts and Galley Items	177
	III. Cabin Items	181
14.	Law Enforcement Response to a Hijacking—What to Expect	185

INTRODUCTION

The information contained in this book might very well help save your life one day. In its original form, it was written as a self-defense manual for aircrew. Since passengers have come to play an increasingly important and necessary role in assisting the aircrew to defend against potential terrorist attacks, we felt that the information in this book would prove to be an invaluable tool for the traveling public as well.

Although specifically written for the airline industry, the information, techniques, and maneuvers found in the following pages can also be effectively applied when traveling on other modes of public transportation should the need arise. However, in this book, we aim to provide you with the information and tools to protect yourself and those around you while aboard an aircraft.

The material contained in this book is by no means all-encompassing. It is virtually impossible to address every situation a flight crew member or passenger may face. The information presented will, however, give both flight crew members and passengers confidence in knowing that they are not "defenseless" in the event of an attack or threat to their personal safety. This book will provide you with some of the basic tools necessary in "de-escalating" minor disturbances, up to and including protection of yourself and those around you.

We realize that many of you have never been exposed to any type of self-defense training. As a matter of fact, most of you may have never even been involved in a fight. With this in mind, our focus is to provide you with some basic "building blocks" of self-defense. As with anything new, you must start at the most basic level. The maneuvers we have included are all very simple and easy to perform.

There are many self-defense books on the market. However, none of them specifically address those maneuvers which can be most effectively executed within the confines of an aircraft. This book aims to fill that gap. Since range of motion is extremely limited on all aircraft, our focus will be on those "close-in," "hand-to-hand" maneuvers which are highly effective in tight places.

We have also included a section at the end of the book which will assist pilots, flight attendants, and passengers in developing the mindset to utilize commonly found objects on an aircraft in order to defend themselves in a hostile situation.

The information contained herein should be reviewed on a regular basis. Long-term memory is best developed through continuous repetition. The techniques that follow, if performed correctly, will cause enough of a delay or distraction so that others on board the aircraft will be able to render assistance.

Remember, there is strength in numbers!

1

A WORD TO PASSENGERS

The events of September 11, 2001 changed the face of air travel forever. Gaining knowledge in self-defense tactics and procedures is one of the best things you can do to aid flight crew members and fellow passengers should a disturbance, potential problem, or terroristic threat occur on the aircraft. If you happen to observe someone behaving suspiciously on the aircraft, immediately notify the nearest uniformed flight crew member. Do not confront the individual yourself! **In all instances, it is imperative that you follow the direction of the flight crew.** Crew members and passengers working together, in an orchestrated manner, will greatly improve the chances of successfully confronting and defeating any threat that may occur on the aircraft. On December 22, 2002, Richard Reid, the infamous "Shoe Bomber," was apprehended on a flight that subsequently diverted into Boston's Logan International Airport. Due to the unified efforts of the flight crew and passengers, Reid was prevented from carrying out his harrowing plan. His ultimate objective was successfully thwarted.

If the flight crew has become incapacitated, however, a unified atmosphere of attack must be created and maintained among the passengers before launching an offensive against potential terrorists or hijackers. A well-thought-out plan will greatly increase the chances for a positive outcome. On

September 11, 2001, passengers on United Flight 93 quickly put together a plan and defeated hijackers on board their aircraft over Pennsylvania. Even though everyone lost their lives in the process, the hijackers were prevented from accomplishing their goal and countless numbers of lives were saved on the ground as a result.

Always remember that there is strength in numbers! Do not act alone! Escalation to mob violence is counterproductive, especially against trained terrorists, and must be avoided.

2

TERRORIST PSYCHOLOGICAL PROFILE

Research on terrorist psychology has yet to reveal a specific psychological type or a uniform mindset that distinguishes terrorists from non-terrorists. Since terrorists do not volunteer for research studies, psychologists who have studied and attempted to define a consistent terrorist psychological profile differ in their opinions of what motivates terrorists. Nevertheless, we present some generally accepted observations on terrorist psychology.

ANGER WITHOUT GUILT

Today's suicide terrorists appear to share the moral and emotional traits exemplified by the Khmer Rouge, who slaughtered thousands of people in Cambodia during the late 1970s. Their definition of right and wrong is dictated by an authoritative figure and is very much "black and white." They are extremely limited in their capacity to think for themselves.

Terrorists develop gradually from a young age. Children, especially boys, and typically aged between ten and sixteen, are the easiest to recruit for suicide terrorism since they are at a developing stage of moral judgment referred to by some psychologists as "retributive justice or vendetta."

Even as adults, terrorists sometimes remain trapped in this stage, with a sense of righteous indignation commonly found among members of paramilitary organizations. Terrorists are very capable of differentiating between right and wrong, yet when it concerns a cause they staunchly believe in, they feel that using violence to defend or support their cause is perfectly justifiable. Boys and girls who adopt this mindset are specifically recruited and nurtured. These "true believers" are angry and feel no guilt about that anger.

THEY ARE RATIONAL

In contrast to the popular sentiment that suicidal terrorists are psychopaths, many experts argue that they are effectively pursuing well-defined goals. As a result, they are considered to be rational and not insane. They have a specific set of goals and their main objective is to work towards achieving those goals. Some psychologists believe that terrorists, as a general rule, tend to have low self-esteem, enjoy taking risks, and are attracted to groups with charismatic and authoritative leaders.

A BRIEF HISTORY

Terrorism first reared its ugly head in Europe during the late 1800s and was generally a quest for "propaganda by deed." For example, terrorists focused their actions on symbols of state power by throwing bombs at czars and other government leaders.

Terrorism resurfaced in the 1960s and 1970s, as some individuals, feeling otherwise powerless, tried to influence or overthrow governments which they considered to be oppressive. Airplane hijackings and large-scale bombings, for the most part, replaced individual assassinations.

Modern terrorism has been described in three waves. The first wave occurred during the 1960s and 1970s, when privately funded organizations, such as the Red Brigade and the Irish Republican Army, concentrated their efforts on individual countries or governments. The second wave took place during the 1970s and 1980s. During this period, terrorist organizations operated internationally under the sponsorship of hostile countries such as Iraq, Iran, Libya, and Syria. The third wave began in the 1990s and continues to the present day. Private organizations, such as Osama Bin Laden's network *(al-Qaeda)*, operate internationally as professional terrorists. Unlike their predecessors, they often use suicide bombers, usually do not take hostages, and typically do not negotiate for concessions. They kill to make a political point but seldom claim responsibility for their acts.

CHANGE IN MOTIVATIONS

In the late 1800s, terrorists engaged in violent activities for a variety of social, psychological, and political reasons. There is evidence to suggest that these early terrorists suffered major damage to their self-image and self-esteem, causing them to search for a new personal identity. Their weakened psychological characteristics made them easy prey for terrorist recruiters. Although these psychological characteristics appear to be significant among earlier terrorists, there is no conclusive evidence to suggest that they are applicable to today's suicide bombers.

The individual psychological factors are not as consistent as they were even a few years ago. Regardless of whether or not their religion condones terrorist actions, modern-day suicide bombers are often motivated by their religious beliefs or by self-interpretation of their faith. Their goal seems to be that of attracting the attention of a deity, rather than the governments and citizens of the countries where their bombs are detonated.

MORE THAN PSYCHOLOGY

Fundamentalist attitudes and characteristics deserve a brief examination, especially in light of the fact that fundamentalist groups have been linked to recent terrorist attacks both in the United States and abroad. Fundamentalist tenets provide followers with strict guidance, and only allow them to see the world in "black and white." There is no "in between." This is one of the major appeals of fundamentalism.

Fundamentalist terrorist groups also offer persuasive inducements to their recruits by telling them that their individual sins and the sins of their families will be forgiven by their God. In addition, Islamic suicide bombers and their families are often seen as heroes in their homelands, and surviving family members are sometimes financially rewarded. As a result, these people are ready and willing to die for their cause.

NO PREDICTABILITY

For law enforcement, identifying and capturing terrorists is not a clear-cut issue. Studies focusing solely on the characteristics of the "criminal" mind versus the "non-criminal" mind, as they pertain to terrorism, have not yielded consistent findings. Experts have not been able to find consistent personality traits which would allow them to predict that one person is more likely to become a terrorist than the next. In order to effectively study the terrorist mentality, we must also take into account their culture, politics, and religion. Without a great deal of further study, psychological profiles and pathological diagnoses are unlikely to provide a satisfying explanation or predictive model for terrorist identification.

3

IDENTIFYING A POTENTIAL PROBLEM/TERRORISTIC THREAT

1. Crew members and passengers must be suspicious and vigilant at all times, especially during the boarding process. As is the case with most neighborhood watch groups, a "nosey" neighbor is a good thing. If something seems strange or out of the ordinary to you, it is worth reporting. Bringing a suspicious matter to the attention of the flight crew is, and always will be, the right thing to do.

2. Be alert for passengers who appear to be:
- unusually nervous
- shifty
- concealing their actions
- covering their hands
- constantly watching the crew's movements
- frequenting the restrooms, especially prior to takeoff
- loitering . . . especially around the forward galley and restroom area
- agitated
- uncooperative
- excessively cooperative

3. Be aware of anyone who appears to be overprotective of his or her luggage, keeping it with him/her at all times, especially when going to the bathroom or moving about the aircraft. Just because someone is constantly clutching his/her bag, it does not make him/her a potential terrorist/hijacker. You should, however, bring it to the attention of a flight crew member.

4. Passengers should notify the nearest crew member if they observe someone acting suspiciously. **They should not approach the person themselves!** Flight crew members should immediately approach any person in question, start up a conversation, and ask as many questions as they can think of. Such questions might include:
- Where are you from?
- What is your final destination?
- Is this a business trip?
- What's your occupation?
- Are you married?
- Do you have kids?
- Can I put your bag in the overhead bin for you?

5. Pay close attention to the responses you receive and the person's associated actions. If after engaging the person in conversation, you find that you are still uncomfortable with the situation, further investigation is urged and strongly recommended. If you are a passenger, you should immediately notify a member of the flight crew if you are suspicious about someone. Are there any law enforcement personnel or air marshals on board who can assist?

6. If the aircraft is already enroute to the destination airport, you must keep the suspicious person in view at all times, paying close attention to his or her every move. **Be discreet!** You do not want to alert this person of your suspicions. Flight attendants should notify the Captain immediately as to the situation at hand. **Serious consideration should be given to landing the aircraft at the nearest airport, while at the same time following company guidelines and procedures.** Are there any law enforcement personnel or air marshals on board who can assist?

NOTE TO AIRCREW MEMBERS:
Do not expose the identity of any law enforcement personnel who may be on board the aircraft. Federal Air Marshals and other law enforcement officers are highly trained to handle these situations and will do so at the appropriate time. Exposing them to the terrorists/hijackers may not only give away their element of surprise but also endanger their lives.

4

PASSENGER REACTIONS

NOTE TO AIRCREW MEMBERS:
If an incident occurs on board the aircraft, you must be ready to deal with both the situation at hand and the various passenger reactions associated with that incident.

Although people respond to events in different ways, their reactions will usually fall into five identifiable categories.

AGGRESSIVE

An aggressive passenger will become involved without crew direction. This person's "Rambo" state of mind will more than likely result in an uncontrolled reaction to the event at hand and could present a danger to those involved in neutralizing the threat. Crew members, especially those not directly involved in the incident, must be aware of and ready to deal with people who react in this manner. Passengers exhibiting this type of behavior need to know that the crew member is in charge.

You must be firm when directing this type of individual. They usually respond well to verbal instructions, and should be given an assignment to channel their excess energy.

PREDICTABLE AND CONTROLLED

This type of passenger will become involved at the direction of crew members and will react to requests in a predictable and controlled manner. People in this category are confident and reasonable in their response to the events at hand and take directions very well. Utilize these individuals by giving them an assignment, especially where you need to have someone who is dependable.

UNPREDICTABLE

As the name implies, passengers falling into this category are unpredictable in their response to a hostile event. They will present a "fight or flight" reaction to the event at hand and may not assist crew members when requested. People falling into this category may initially engage the threat, but quickly retreat, leaving crew members to fend for themselves. If they have assumed a role in the event, be prepared to replace them. Do not depend on this type of individual for "high-risk" assignments.

SYMPATHETIC

Passengers suffering from a condition known as the "Stockholm syndrome" will develop an emotional bond and become sympathetic with the perpetrators. In some instances, they may even side with the perpetrators and take up their cause. You may need to assign someone to watch this type of person. Expect them to be emotional. Do not include these individuals in planning or decision-making roles. People exhibiting this type of behavior pose a threat to those crew members attempting to deal with the situation at hand and should, if at all possible, be relocated to a different area of the cabin.

"DO NOTHINGS"

These passengers will not engage in any way because of their inability to control their fear. They may, however, react unpredictably and become an additional problem for crew members, by adding uncontrolled vocal outbursts to an already volatile situation. Should they exhibit this type of behavior, these individuals should be removed from the area of engagement so as not to hinder the crew member's efforts in dealing with the situation at hand. Be prepared to deal firmly with this type of person.

5

CRISIS MANAGEMENT

In any situation, it is absolutely essential that a crew member take charge and direct actions to maintain order. Should an incident arise, following the crew position pecking order is an excellent place to start: captain, first officer, #1 flight attendant, #2 flight attendant, #3 flight attendant, etc. Should a situation develop in the cabin . . . **always keep the captain informed! Flight crews should create a unified atmosphere of attack. Escalation to "mob violence" must not be allowed!**

* IT IS IMPERATIVE THAT PASSENGERS FOLLOW THE DIRECTION OF UNIFORMED CREW MEMBERS! IF THE FLIGHT CREW IS INCAPACITATED, PASSENGERS SHOULD DEVISE A PLAN IN ORDER TO CREATE A UNIFIED ATMOSPHERE OF ATTACK! IF AT ALL POSSIBLE, YOUR PLAN OF ATTACK MUST BE COVERTLY PLANNED. REMEMBER, THESE TYPES OF PLANS SHOULD ONLY BE CARRIED OUT AS A LAST RESORT IN ORDER TO SAVE BOTH THE AIRCRAFT AND THE LIVES OF THOSE ABOARD.

DEFINITION

REASONABLE OR NECESSARY FORCE:

The minimum amount of lawful aggression sufficient to achieve a legitimate lawful objective.

6

USE OF FORCE FACTORS

You must first analyze the situation and ask yourself the following questions:
1. What is the nature of the threat?
2. Is the subject acting aggressively?
3. Is the subject armed?

After analyzing the situation, crew members and passengers should act with the appropriate level of force as deemed necessary according to the guidelines established in the **Levels of Force Continuum** located on page 21. To use the Continuum correctly, begin with the lowest level of force appropriate to the situation, progressing from Level I to Level III as necessary. In every situation, crew and passengers must be firm and prepared to protect themselves by using only the force necessary to neutralize the situation. Keep in mind that we do not advocate "vigilante" force. Our only interest is the protection of both the aircraft and the lives of those aboard. Some measures should only be used as a last resort.

Force must be used wisely. As the subject's level of aggression increases, so does the level of force used to counter that aggression. As the subject's level of aggression decreases, so does the level of force. Always keep in mind that words and gestures alone do not constitute a physical attack. Safety of the crew and passengers is paramount!

It is important to note that if you determine the incident is a life-threatening, terroristic threat, the first two levels of the Continuum do not apply. If you are in a deadly situation, talking will do no good! You must immediately assume a "warrior" mindset. Your best defense, in this instance, is to plan a "takedown" using the techniques that are explained in this book under Level III of the Continuum. Understand that in the process, you may get injured. However, injury is a more preferable alternative than losing your life. If the maneuver you are attempting to perform is not working, quickly move to another. **As you are working the maneuvers, it is essential that you "yell out" and enlist the aid of others on board the aircraft. Remember, there is strength in numbers!**

7

LEVELS OF FORCE CONTINUUM

I. Professional Presence

↓

II. Verbal Communications

↓

III. Physical Contact

I. Professional Presence

1. A uniformed crew member entering a situation is sometimes enough to change the course of events and quell a potential uprising.

2. A uniformed crew member entering a situation with one or more passengers at his or her side may also quell a potential uprising.

Note to aircrew members: Remember to be professional, firm, confident, composed, and calm.

II. Verbal Communications

1. Attempt to use words in order to gain control of a potentially hostile situation. Our goal is to redirect behavior with words in order to generate voluntary compliance.

2. Golden Rule: Always treat others the way you would want to be treated. (Keep in mind that a terrorist/hijacker does not care about the "Golden Rule.")

3. Stay composed and calm.

4. Read the scene:
- Analyze the problem
- What kind of obstacles are you dealing with?

5. Ask questions to:
- Force the other person to stop talking and listen
- Demonstrate concern
- Gain control by causing others to report to you
- Direct attention away from the problem
- Buy time
- Find out facts and seek opinions to understand the person's mindset

6. Listen carefully to the responses you receive:
- Listening is a skill that must be developed
- Listening is a combination of hearing what the other person is saying and being involved with the person who is talking

7. Verbally respond back to the subject in order to:
- Summarize
  Repeat what you have learned in your own words. Sometimes, this minimizes the demands made by the subject. **(Your summary must be brief, concise, and above all, inarguable.)**
- Ensure that you understand the situation
- Show that you are truly listening

8. Think before you speak! Don't just blurt out whatever comes to mind!

9. Some potentially confrontational statements one should **never** include in a response:
- "COME HERE"
- "YOU WOULDN'T UNDERSTAND"
- "BECAUSE THOSE ARE THE RULES"
- "IT'S NONE OF YOUR BUSINESS"
- "WHAT DO YOU WANT ME TO DO ABOUT IT?"
- "WHAT'S YOUR PROBLEM?"
- "I'M NOT GOING TO SAY THIS AGAIN"
- "I'M DOING THIS FOR YOUR OWN GOOD"
- "THE EASY WAY OR THE HARD WAY"

10. Some potentially confrontational trigger words one should **never** include in a response:
- "YOU PEOPLE"
- "HEY YOU"
- "HEY PAL"

- "HEY BUBBA"
- "DUDE"
- "CHILL OUT"
- "OR ELSE"
- "SO"

11. Once you understand the problem you are dealing with, concentrate on calming the subject through the use of verbal appeals.
   Here are four types of verbal appeals.

   A. ETHICAL APPEAL :

   An attempt to gain credibility and trustworthiness by appealing to a person's principles of right and wrong. This type of appeal is useful when dealing with people who are upset and highly emotional.
   Can be effective if:
   - appeal is made by someone in a position of authority, like a professional crew member
   - appeal strikes a chord with the person's beliefs and value system
   - it persuades others of your desire for a positive outcome
   - it assures the other person

   B. PERSONAL APPEAL:

   An attempt to gain credibility and trustworthiness by appealing to a person's individual needs and desires. This kind of appeal works well with headstrong people who insist on getting their own way.

However, you may have to set aside your own personal values when dealing with this type of person.

C. Practical Appeal:

An attempt to gain credibility and trustworthiness by adapting yourself to the situation and persuading the other person that you are like them. This kind of appeal is best used in a situation where there is an urgent need to change a particular circumstance.

It is important to remember that a practical appeal is a short-term solution that ignores long-term consequences.

D. Rational Appeal:

An attempt to gain credibility and trustworthiness by appealing to a person's common sense and good judgment, or sense of community standards.

This kind of appeal is useful when dealing with people who have a strong sense of right and wrong.
- Based on use of reasoning
- Show that solution is reasonable and most likely to produce results

III. PHYSICAL CONTACT

1. Physical contact may need to be used when words are no longer working and the threat is perceived to be real.

2. When a person seriously threatens bodily harm, control is compromised.

3. Sometimes an agitated person combines aggressive words with actions. **(Remember—words and gestures alone are not an attack.)**

4. Sometimes an agitated person displays conflicting signs. Words suggest one thing and actions suggest another. A good principle to remember is: **When words and actions disagree, trust actions.** For example, a person may be very cooperative. However, his or her physical signs indicate that an attack may be imminent.

5. Actions can also be misleading, but whenever words and actions disagree, be alert and ready to use force.

6. Signs that a person is about to become violent or physical:
   - They tell you that they're ready to "whip you"
   - They assume a fighting or martial arts stance
   - They look to see if anyone is paying attention
   - Clenching of fists
   - Fist in palm
   - Gritting teeth
   - Growling/screaming
   - Rocking back and forth

- Bobbing up and down
- Shoulder shift
- "1000 yard" stare or distant look

8

CONCEPTS OF CLOSE QUARTER TACTICS

1. **SITUATIONAL AWARENESS**
   - Be suspicious and vigilant at all times.
   - Be aware that a distraction or diversion could be used as a "set-up" for something to occur in another area.
   - Keep the subject or subjects in question in view at all times, paying close attention to their every move.

2. **SPEED**
   - Speed is essential in order to successfully subdue a subject.
   - Movements should be automatic so that you react quickly.
   - Initial training on the tactics in this book should concentrate on precision and accuracy of movement. Speed will come through practice and constant review.

3. **SURPRISE**
   - There is no greater advantage than the element of surprise.
   - The element of surprise can be achieved by the combined effects of yelling at your opponent, speed, and accuracy of movement.
   - The subject will be stunned and caught off guard when faced with someone who is well prepared.

4. **LEVERAGE**

    - In every case, it must be assumed that you are not as strong as your opponent.
    - Even if you perceive that you are stronger, never go "head-to-head" with your opponent to test his or her strength.
    - Use your opponent's momentum to effectively gain leverage.

5. **BALANCE**

    - Maintain balance at all times by keeping feet "shoulder width" apart.
    - Work to cause your opponent to lose balance by pushing, pulling, tripping, etc., thereby gaining leverage.
    - Maintaining balance is absolutely essential to the successful outcome of a conflict.

9

TARGET AREAS OF THE HUMAN BODY

NOTE: Use extreme caution when practicing strikes to the target areas shown on pages 32–33. It takes very little pressure or force directed at those areas to cause serious injury or death.

TARGET AREAS

EYES
NOSE
EARS
CHIN
SIDE OF NECK
COLLAR BONE
BASE OF THROAT
ARMPIT
ELBOW
FLOATING RIBS
GROIN
FINGERS
FEMORAL NERVE
KNEE

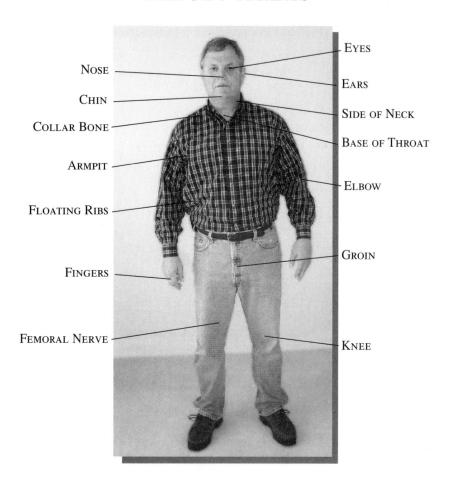

TARGET AREAS

TEMPLE
UPPER LIP
ADAM'S APPLE
SOLAR PLEXUS
STOMACH
WRIST
IN STEP
NAPE
SHOULDER
SPINE
KIDNEY
ANKLE

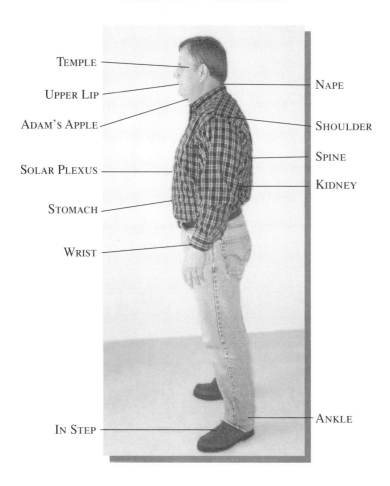

10

CLOSE QUARTER MANEUVERS AND TACTICS

The maneuvers that follow have been carefully chosen because of their effectiveness in "tight" areas. They are all very basic and easy to perform. Some of the maneuvers may seem severe; however, if an incident progresses to the point of physical contact, you are in a life-or-death situation and extreme measures must be taken to ensure the safety of the crew and passengers. An aggressor must be disabled, especially when airborne, or else he or she will continue to pursue. All of the techniques that follow can be accomplished from either the left hand side or the right hand side.

THOSE MANEUVERS THAT MAY CAUSE SERIOUS INJURY OR POSSIBLY EVEN DEATH HAVE BEEN ANNOTATED BY AN ASTERISK (*).

NOTE: Control techniques, which are mentioned in some maneuvers, are defined as "flex cuffing" a person by utilizing a nylon cable tie or tying a person's hands with a dress tie, belt, etc. The person may then be confined to a seat using a seat belt.

I. Weapons of the Body
[HANDS]
A. Bladed Hand

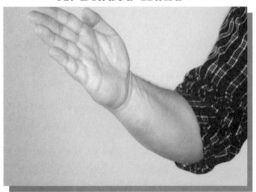

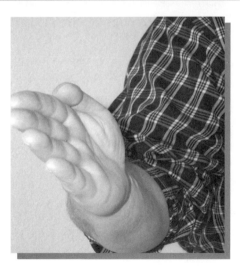

Fingers must be rigidly extended. The thumb must be kept tucked alongside the forefinger.

B. Fists

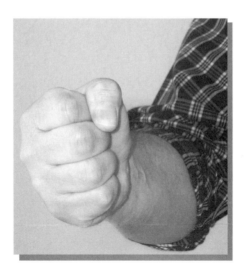

Fingers folded at the second knuckle. (This results in a more effective, penetrating blow.) Wrist held straight. Thumb held firmly against the forefinger.

B. Fists (continued)

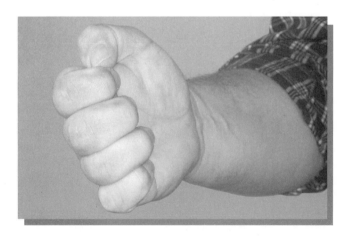

Fingers folded at the second knuckle.
Wrist held straight.

B. Fists (continued)

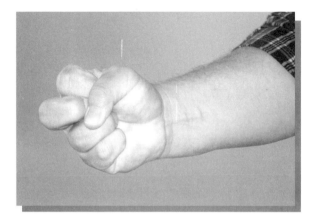

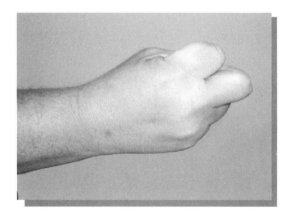

Similar to the pictures on the previous page; however, the second knuckle of the middle finger is protruding outward. The second knuckle of the adjacent fingers should be wedged into the middle finger with the thumb tucked over the fingernail of the middle finger. Wrist held straight.

C. Heel of Hand

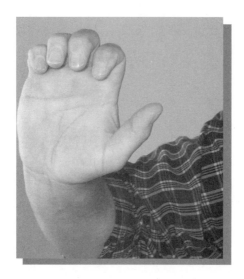

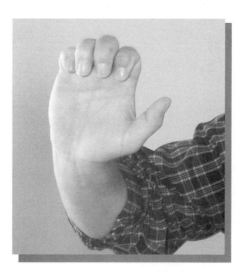

Fingers folded at the second knuckle with the hand bent back toward the wrist.

D. Fingers

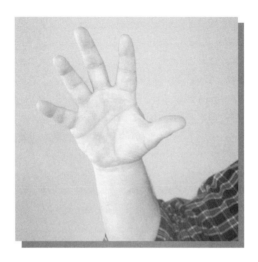

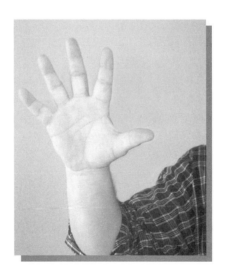

Used to grab, gouge, rip, scratch, and poke.

E. Forearms

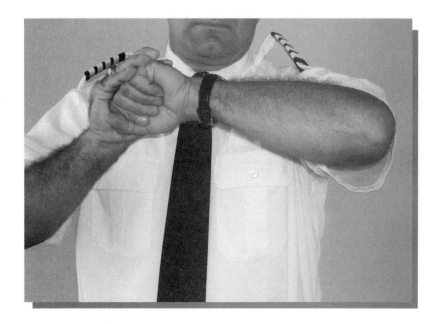

Can be used very effectively as a blocking/deflecting tool. Can also be used to strike or deliver blows.

CLOSE QUARTER MANEUVERS AND TACTICS

F. Elbows

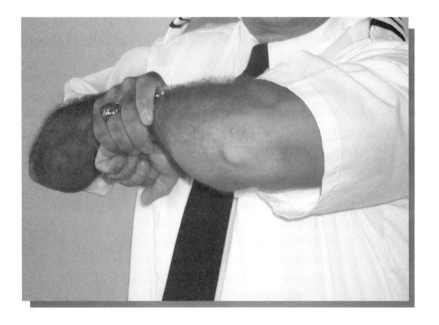

Very effective and powerful weapon in close range situations when used to strike or deliver blows.

G. Legs

1. Feet

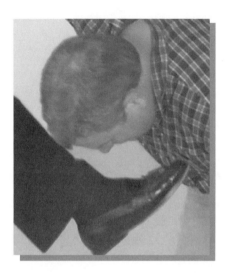

When kicking, use outside edge or inside edge of shoe. Can also use the heel to stomp an opponent or rake his/her shins. Kicks may also be accomplished using the toes, as long as a shoe of some type is worn.

2. Knees

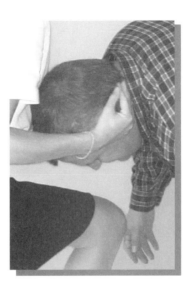

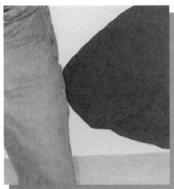
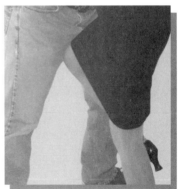

As with elbows, knees are very effective in close range situations when used to strike blows. The most effective target areas when using the knee as a weapon include the groin and face (if the opponent is bent over).

II. STANCES

A. Recommended Stance for Defusing a Situation

B. Defensive or Self-Protection Stance

III. Strikes

> It is recommended that strikes be accomplished by utilizing the fist, forearm, heel of the palm, bladed hand, elbow, or fingers. Study the following pictures to understand how these striking methods are performed.

A. Palm Heel Strike to the Face*

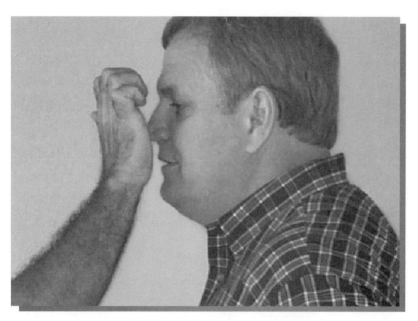

B. Forearm to the Side of the Neck*

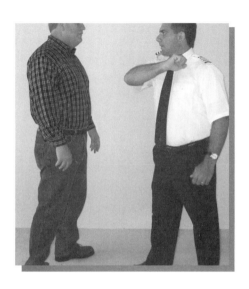

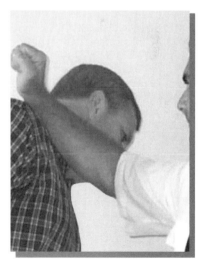

C. Strike to the Throat*

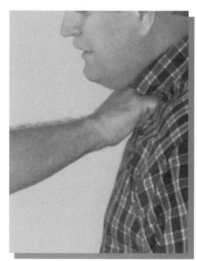

D. Round House Punch or Slap

E. Straight Punch

F. Back Arm Strike to Side of the Neck*
(Used against a violent person . . . this will knock the person out.)

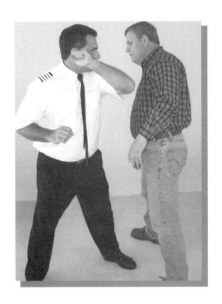

G. Inside Arm Strike to the Side of the Neck*
(Used against a violent person . . . this will knock the person out.)

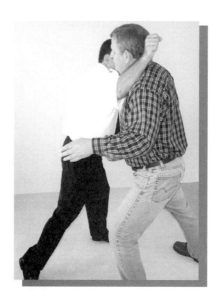

H. Back Hand Slap to the Side of the Neck
(This will cause a person to become disoriented.)

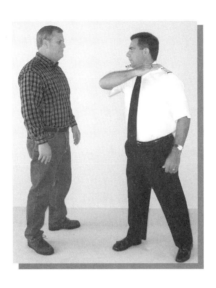

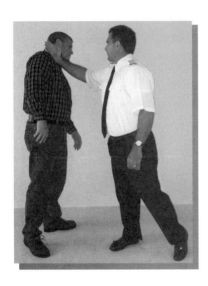

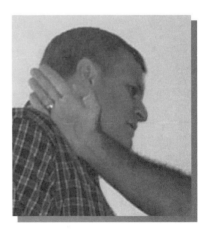

IV. Blocks

A. Round House Punch and Associated Block

Note: Blocking should be done with the forearm. Always keep your other hand "up and ready" in order to protect yourself should the subject strike with the opposite hand.

CLOSE QUARTER MANEUVERS AND TACTICS

B. Straight Punch and Associated Block or Parry

C. Kick to the Groin and Associated Cross Block

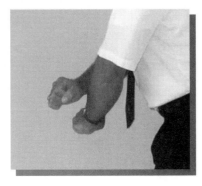

CLOSE QUARTER MANEUVERS AND TACTICS

C. Kick to the Groin and Associated Cross Block
(continued)

V. GROUND FIGHTING TECHNIQUES

A. Ear Slaps

Ear slaps are used to cause a mental stunning and pain compliance. When used properly, the ear slap will cause pain and disorientation. Ear slaps are also used as a distraction technique. (See Attempted Front Choke Hold, page 104)

1. Cup both hands and deliver as if throwing a round house punch.

A. Ear Slaps (continued)

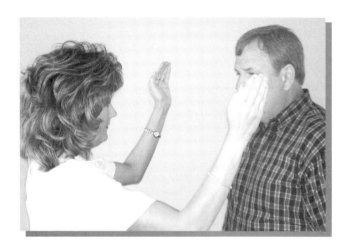

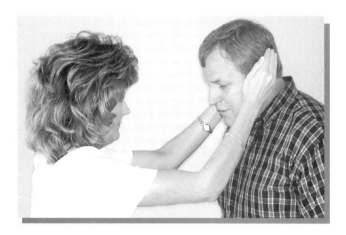

2. Slap the ears of the assailant with cupped hands.

A. Ear Slaps (continued)

3. Follow up with a control technique.

B. Eye Flicks*

Eye flicks may be used to temporarily disable a hostile person. The eye flick will cause severe lacrimation and a scar on the eyeball. This can be performed with either the left or the right hand.

1. The wrist should be limp.

B. Eye Flicks (continued)

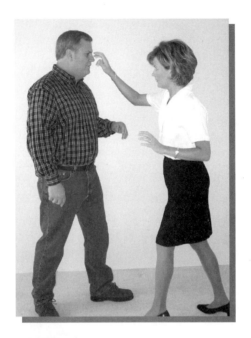

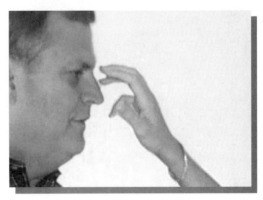

2. With the fingers extended, flick the hands at the eyes of the assailant.

C. Eye Gouges*

Eye gouges can cause serious damage and possibly loss of sight.

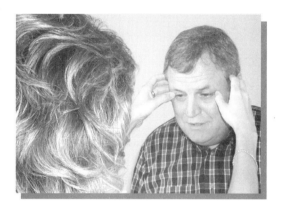

> Push the thumb or any finger into the eye. The thumb/finger can then be worked around to the back of the eyeball in order to pull the eyeball out of its socket.

C. Eye Gouges (continued)

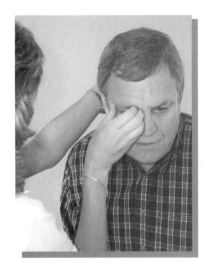

CLOSE QUARTER MANEUVERS AND TACTICS

D. Groin Squeeze

A groin squeeze will temporarily disable an offender. This technique utilizes pain compliance. You should exert a maximum amount of force when utilizing this technique. Do not stop until the assailant falls to the ground or begins to get sick.

> With either hand, firmly grab the genitalia of the assailant and squeeze. (Follow up with a control technique.)
> **Note:** This maneuver may also be performed as a groin strike.

E. Head Butts

Head butts should be utilized as a distraction. This technique utilizes pain compliance and will redirect the thought processes of an assailant. Head butts can be performed with the top front, sides, or back of the head. **It is important that you not utilize your forehead!**

1. When face to face with an assailant, tilt your head forward and down.
2. As fast as you can, while pulling his head toward you, thrust your head into the nose area of the assailant. Follow up with a control technique.

E. Head Butts (continued)

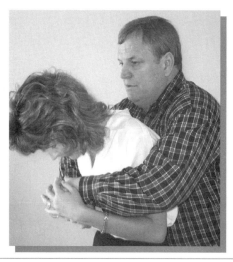

1. When the assailant is behind you, put your chin on your chest. (A "knuckle rap" on the back of the assailant's hands may also cause loss of grip.)

2. Thrust the back of your head into the nose area of the assailant. (Follow up with a control technique.)

F. Lip Pulls

Lip pulls allow you to control a subject. This technique will not cause serious damage. It is a control technique that utilizes pain compliance.

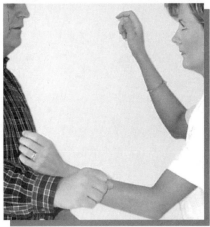

1. With either hand . . .

F. Lip Pulls (continued)

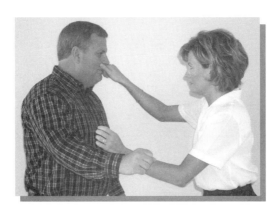

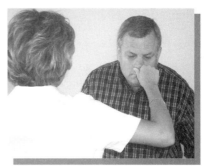

2. Grasp the upper lip of an unruly person with the thumb and forefinger.
Do not put your hand in the person's mouth!

F. Lip Pulls (continued)

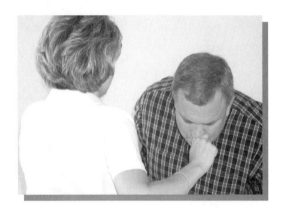

3. With a downward pull, you will be able to lead the person to the ground or to another control technique.

G. Throat Grab*

Throat grabs should be used in an encounter in which an assailant is attempting serious bodily injury or death. **This is a pain compliance technique that will disable and possibly cause death.**

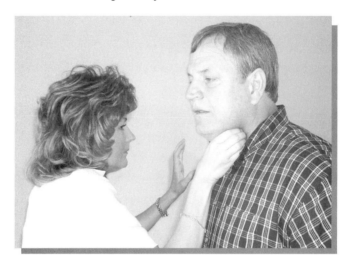

1. With your strong hand, grab the throat of the assailant.

G. Throat Grab (continued)

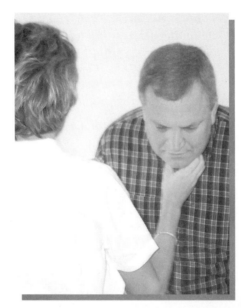

2. Squeeze with as much force as you can muster, then pull. Release when the assailant is disabled.

VI. Kicks/Knee Strikes

A. Foot Stomps

The foot stomp is a disabling technique that utilizes pain compliance. It can also be used to distract. It only takes three pounds of pressure to break the bone on the top of the foot.

With either foot, stomp downward on top of the assailant's foot.

B. Knee Strikes

Knee strikes have proven to be very effective in disabling a hostile person by utilizing pain compliance. Knee strikes can also be used as a distraction technique. The most effective areas to strike are the groin, the nerve on the side of the leg and the femoral nerve on the inside of the leg. (See Target Areas of the Human Body, pages 31-33.)

Knee Strike to the Thigh

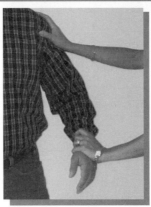

1. Step back as far as practical on the leg you will be using to perform this strike.

Knee Strike to the Thigh (continued)

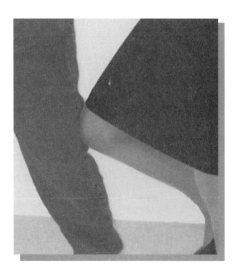

2. With as much force as possible, utilizing the hard bony part of your knee, strike the target area.

Knee Strike to the Groin

1. Step back, as far as practical, on the leg you will be using to perform this strike.

Knee Strike to the Groin (continued)

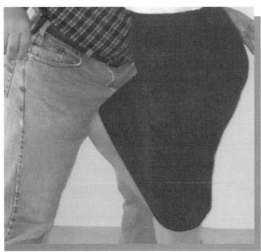

2. With as much force as possible, utilizing the hard bony part of the knee, strike the target area.

C. Shin Kick/Shin Rake

Shin kicks and shin rakes can be used on someone attacking from the front or the rear. They are very effective in stopping an aggressive person from coming toward you. They can also be used as distraction techniques. The pictures shown below depict a person attacking from behind.

Shin Kick

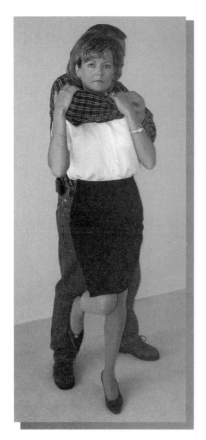
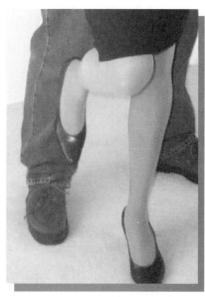

Utilizing the side of your foot, kick the shin area of the assailant with as much force as is possible. (Follow up with a control technique.)

Shin Rake

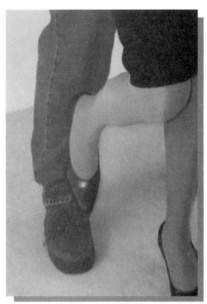

Utilizing the side of your foot, scrape the shin area of the assailant's leg with a quick, downward motion. (Follow up with a control technique.)

Shin Rake (continued)

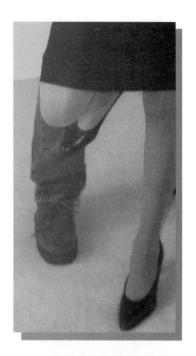

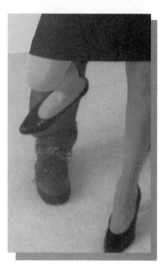

D. Grabs
Finger/Thumb Spread*

This technique allows you to control a subject by utilizing pain compliance. **This technique can cause finger and thumb damage.**

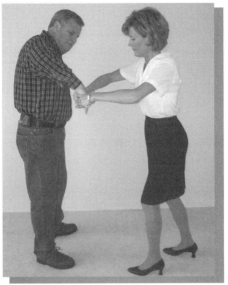

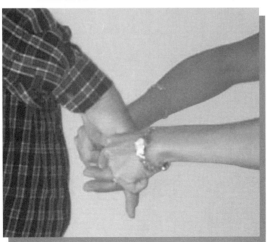

1. Grab the thumb and small finger on the same hand.

Finger/Thumb Spread (continued)

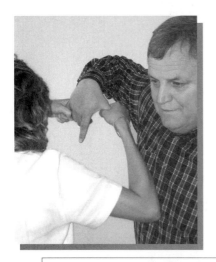
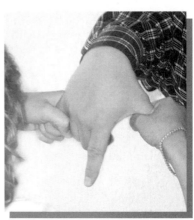

2. Spread the thumb and small finger apart and at the same time . . .

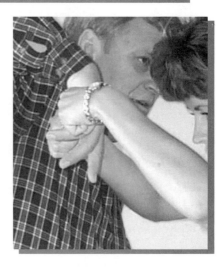

3. Take the subject's hand toward his/her shoulder, elevating the elbow on the hand you are controlling.

Wrist Trap

In the event that someone grabs you by the shirt and attempts to control you or harm you, this technique will allow you to disengage and take the subject to the ground. This technique relies on pain compliance.

1. Grab the subject's hand with your strong hand, trapping him/her so that he/she cannot pull away. Keep the hand close to your body.

Wrist Trap (continued)

2. With your other hand, grab the subject's trapped hand underneath, keeping the hand next to your body.

Wrist Trap (continued)

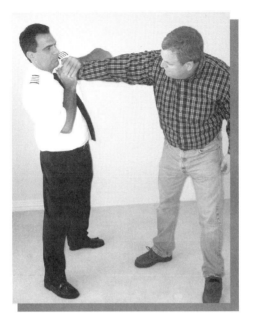

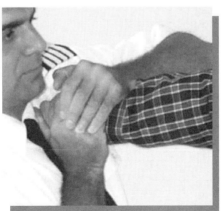

3. Rotate the subject's hand so that the little finger is pointing upward.

Wrist Trap (continued)

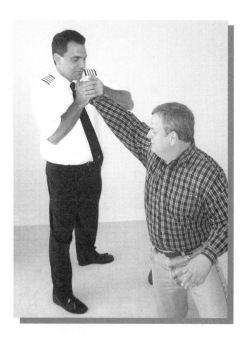

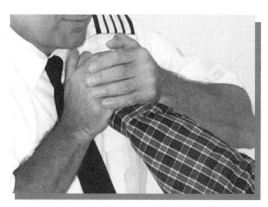

4. Apply pressure toward the subject's now-extended arm, keeping his/her hand trapped against your body.

Wrist Trap (continued)

5. Follow up with kick to the face.

E. Pressure Point Tactic

This technique relies on pressure with counter-pressure. If a person is uncooperative, hostile, and non-compliant . . .

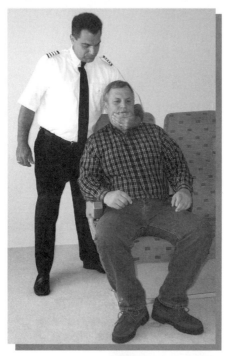

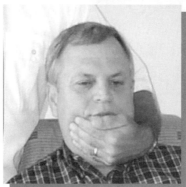

1. Grab the person around the head as shown above.

Pressure Point Tactic (continued)

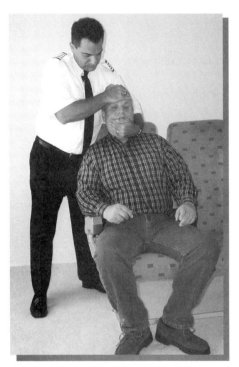

2. Hold the person's head steady by grabbing his forehead with your opposite hand.

Pressure Point Tactic (continued)

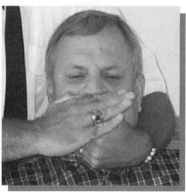

3. Blade the hand you just used in the previous step to steady the person's head and press on top of the upper lip just below the nose.

Pressure Point Tactic (continued)

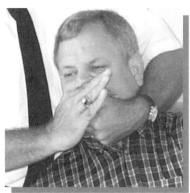

4. Push sharply toward the nose. This will cause pain and make the eyes water.

F. Grip Breaks

An unruly or hostile person may grab hold of something or someone and refuse to release his or her grip . . .

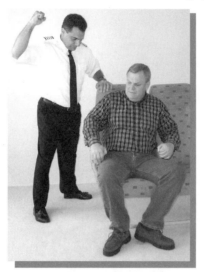

1. Hammer fist the person on top of the arm as shown above.

Grip Breaks (continued)

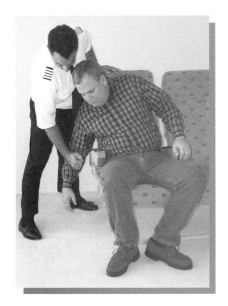

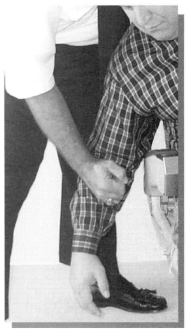

2. This creates pain and causes the person to release his grip.

Grip Breaks (continued)

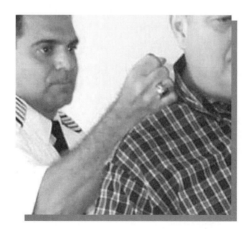

1. A hammer fist to the top of the shoulder blade will also cause pain . . .

Grip Breaks (continued)

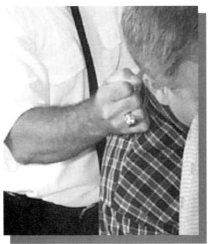

2. And cause the person to let go of his or her grip.

G. Front Choke Hold

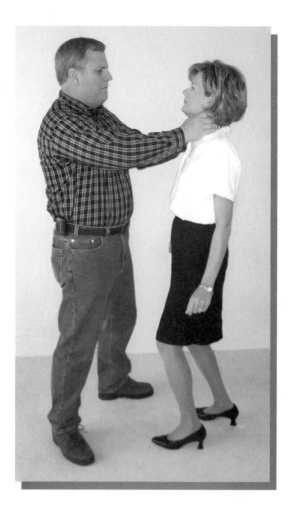

1. If the attacker performs a front choke hold as shown above . . .

Front Choke Hold (continued)

2. Throw your arms straight up and scream.

Front Choke Hold (continued)

3. Turn your body at a 45-degree angle.

Front Choke Hold (continued)

4. Elbow strike the attacker's arm.

Front Choke Hold (continued)

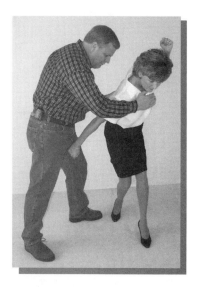
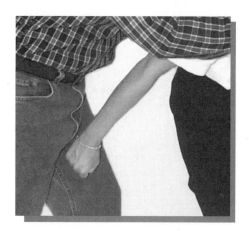

5. Apply a hammer fist to the groin.

H. Attempted Front Choke Hold

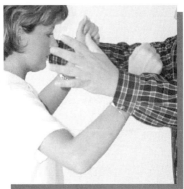

1. If the attacker is coming toward you in the manner depicted above, block both arms of the attacker.

Attempted Front Choke Hold (continued)

2. Perform an ear slap.

CLOSE QUARTER MANEUVERS AND TACTICS

Attempted Front Choke Hold (continued)

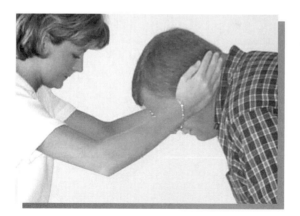

3. Pull the attacker's head straight down.

Attempted Front Choke Hold (continued)

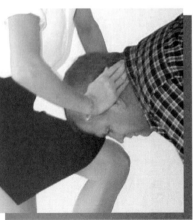

4. Knee strike him to the face, then disengage.

I. Rear Choke Hold, Variation #1

1. If the attacker is attacking from behind, as depicted above . . .

Note: As a first line of defense, attempt to tuck your chin against your chest, thus making it difficult for the attacker to get his arm around your throat.

Rear Choke Hold, Variation #1 (continued)

2. Perform a foot stomp. (It only takes three pounds of pressure to break the bone on the top of the foot.) If unable to reach or find the attacker's foot, perform a shin rake. (See pages 81–82.)

Rear Choke Hold, Variation #1 (continued)

3. Perform a hammer fist to the groin.

Rear Choke Hold, Variation #1 (continued)

4. Push the attacker's elbow upward as shown, while maintaining a firm grip on his arm, and simultaneously step behind the attacker.

Rear Choke Hold, Variation #1 (continued)

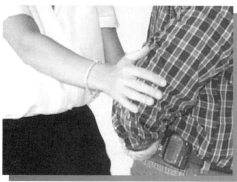

5. Apply a wrist lock, as shown above.

J. Rear Choke Hold, Variation #2

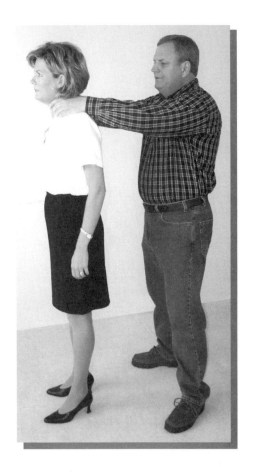

1. If the attacker does a throat grab from behind . . .

Rear Choke Hold, Variation #2 (continued)

2. Throw your arms straight up and scream.

Rear Choke Hold, Variation #2 (continued)

3. Turn your body at a 45-degree angle to the attacker.

Rear Choke Hold, Variation #2 (continued)

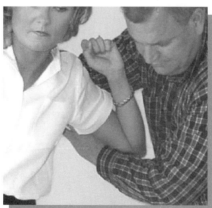

4. Bring your elbow downward, firmly striking the top of the attacker's arm, thus causing him to release his grip.

Rear Choke Hold, Variation #2 (continued)

5. Apply a hammer fist to the groin.

K. Headlock

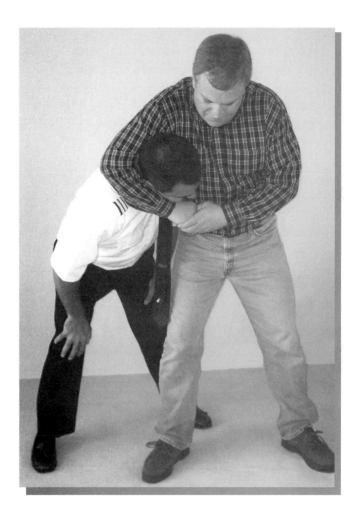

1. If an attacker gets you into a headlock . . .

Headlock (continued)

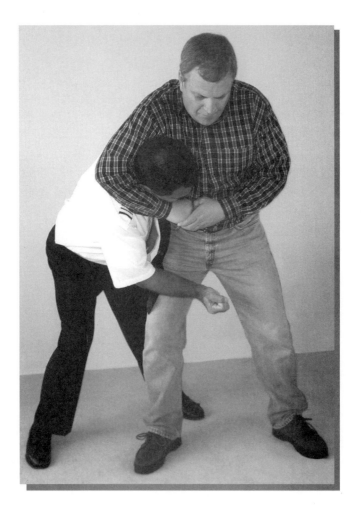

2. Apply a hammer fist to the groin.

Headlock (continued)

3. Step in front of the attacker with your leg that is closest to him.

Headlock (continued)

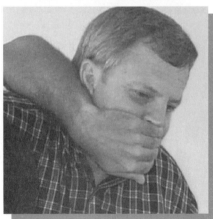

4. Reach around from behind and grab the eyes, hair, or under the nose of the attacker.

Headlock (continued)

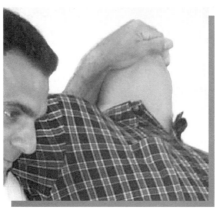

5. Pull back and down sharply.
(This will cause him to lose his grip.)

L. Single Wrist Grab

1. When an attacker grabs your wrist as depicted above . . .

Single Wrist Grab (continued)

2. Trap the attacker's hand using your free hand so that he can't escape and . . .

Single Wrist Grab (continued)

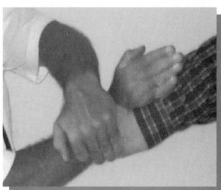

3. Simultaneously rotate your wrist, thereby forcing the attacker's little finger to point upward and torque his wrist toward, or into, his body.

Single Wrist Grab (continued)

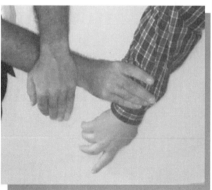

4. This will cause great pain, thus forcing the attacker to release his grip.

M. Dual Wrist Grab

1. When an attacker grabs both wrists as depicted above . . .

Dual Wrist Grab (continued)

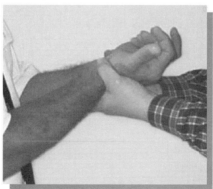

2. **With a quick jerking motion,** pull your arms up while simultaneously rotating your hands outward toward the thumbs of the attacker.

Dual Wrist Grab (continued)

3. This should release the attacker's grip.

Dual Wrist Grab (continued)

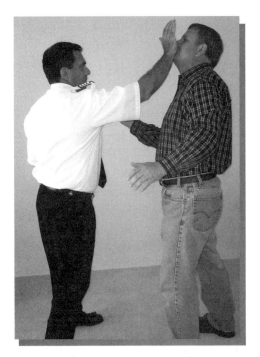

4. Follow up with a palm heel strike to the face.

N. Wrist Lock Come Along

1. While attempting to escort an **unruly** individual away from others . . .

Wrist Lock Come Along (continued)

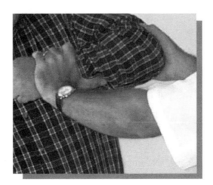

2. The individual reacts and bends his elbow, holding it tight against his body.

Wrist Lock Come Along (continued)

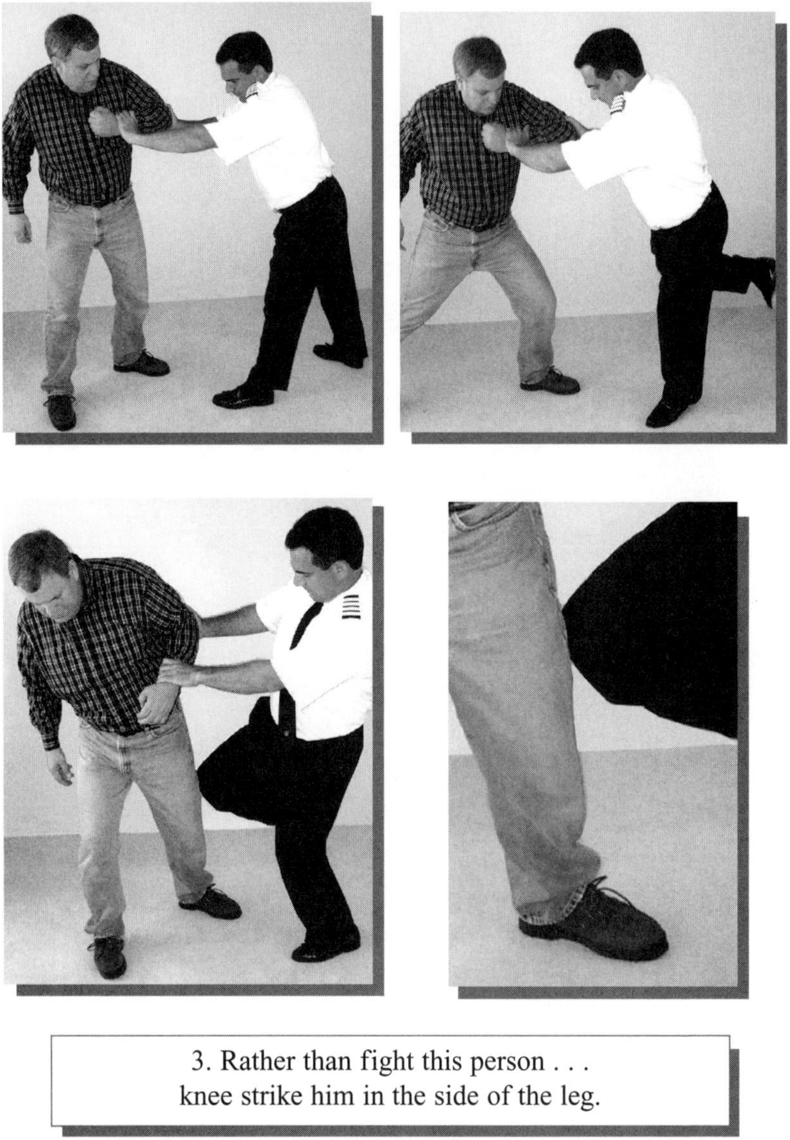

3. Rather than fight this person . . .
knee strike him in the side of the leg.

Wrist Lock Come Along (continued)

4. With your right hand, pull his elbow into the pit of your arm.

Wrist Lock Come Along (continued)

5. Bend the wrist down and apply pressure.

Wrist Lock Come Along (continued)

6. Elevate the wrist.

11

WEAPON TAKEAWAYS

It should be noted that it is very dangerous to disarm someone wielding a knife, box cutter, or gun. Disarming techniques should be utilized as a last resort. Many times a hostage taker will not harm you if you cooperate. In most hostage situations, the more time that goes by, the less likely it is that you will be harmed. Only you can determine what to do and when to react.

Anyone attempting these techniques must have a survival attitude and a "warrior" mindset. In other words, a person must believe that he or she will be successful.

When taking a knife or box cutter away from someone, **it is extremely important to observe how the attacker is holding the knife/box cutter.** Expect to be cut. If you do get cut and see blood, don't panic and let it distract you! A cut on the outside of the arm or on the hand will not cause death. **Remember, it is better to suffer a cut than to lose your life.**

When utilizing gun or knife/box cutter takeaways, you must continue with the maneuver until you have control of the weapon. Understand that this may mean having to withstand blows to your body in order to realize a successful outcome.

The techniques discussed in the following pages are simple and easily mastered and should be practiced on a regular basis. **NEVER practice gun, knife, or box cutter takeaways with real weapons! "Dummy" guns and knives can be purchased at a relatively low cost through various outlets. Box cutter takeaways should be practiced with the blade(s) removed.**

> **CAUTION:** When practicing the gun takeaway maneuvers, the person holding the gun should keep his or her finger **"OFF"** the trigger. Loss of limb or serious injury could result if the finger is in the trigger housing during the takeaway.

I. Gun Takeaways

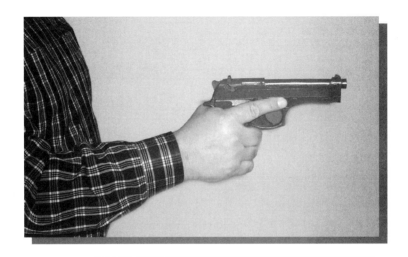

Example of pointed gun with finger **off** trigger.

Example of pointed gun with finger **on** trigger.

A. Gun Pointed at the Chest or Midsection

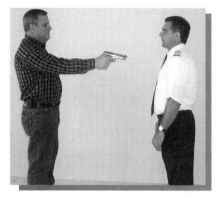

1. Gun aimed at crew member's chest, finger on the trigger.

2. Always put your hands up . . . even if the attacker does not ask you to. Keep your hands gun level. Never reach higher than the gun.

WEAPON TAKEAWAYS

Gun Pointed at the Chest or Midsection (continued)

3. Grab the gun while simultaneously turning your upper body. By turning your body, you make yourself a smaller target. Speed and quickness is of utmost importance when accomplishing this step.

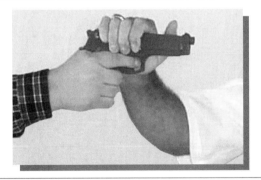

Note 1: If the attacker is holding the gun in his left hand, grab the gun with your left hand. If the subject is holding the gun in his right hand, grab the gun with your right hand. This will ensure that the attacker will turn the gun loose when you complete the technique.

Gun Pointed at the Chest or Midsection (continued)

SLIDE

Note 2: With a semi-automatic weapon, you will be grabbing the slide in order to lock it up and cause a jam.

WEAPON TAKEAWAYS

Gun Pointed at the Chest or Midsection (continued)

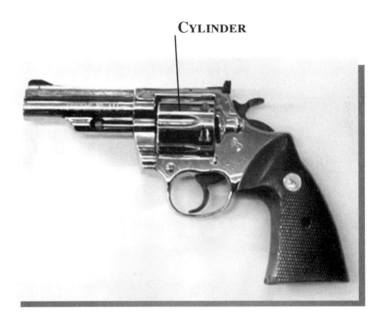

Note 3: With a revolver, you will be grabbing the cylinder in order to keep it from rotating. The revolver cannot be fired when the cylinder is locked up.

Gun Pointed at the Chest or Midsection (continued)

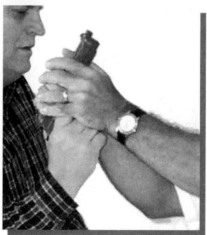

4. With your free hand, grab your hand that is on the weapon. This will add strength and support.

Gun Pointed at the Chest or Midsection (continued)

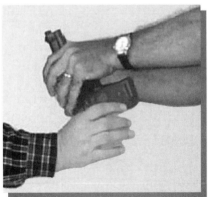

5. Step in, toward the attacker, while simultaneously turning the barrel of the weapon toward him. This will create pain in his hand and wrist. It is extremely important that you maintain a firm grip on the gun. **DO NOT LET GO!** His hand will open and he will turn the gun loose.

Gun Pointed at the Chest or Midsection (continued)

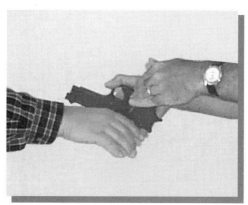

6. Step back and away from the attacker with the gun.

B. Gun Pointed at the Head

1. Gun aimed at crew member's head.

Gun Pointed at the Head (continued)

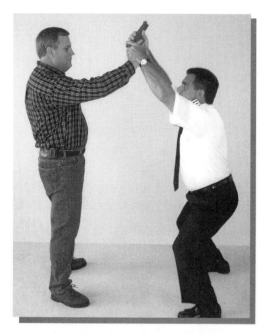

2. Drop down and simultaneously grab the gun with both hands pushing upward.

Gun Pointed at the Head (continued)

3. Turn the barrel of the gun toward the attacker. His hand will open, thus releasing the grip.

II. KNIFE/BOX CUTTER TAKEAWAYS

A. Knife/Box Cutter Takeaway #1 Stab

1. If an attacker is attempting to stab you in the manner depicted above . . .

Knife/Box Cutter Takeaway #1 Stab (continued)

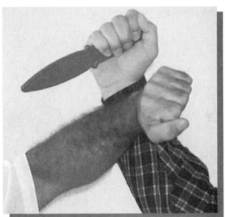

2. Use your forearm to block the attacker's arm as it is coming toward you in a downward motion. Mirror yourself to the attacker. Always block with the arm that is on the same side as the attacker's stabbing arm. In other words, if the attacker stabs with his right hand, block with your left forearm. If he stabs with his left hand, block with your right forearm.

Knife/Box Cutter Takeaway #1 Stab (continued)

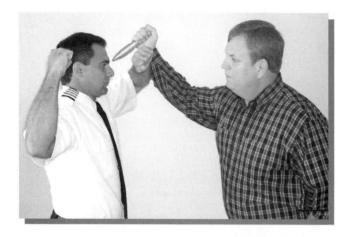

3. Make a hard fist with your free hand . . .

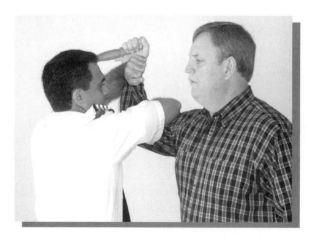

4. Strike the attacker's arm at the bend in the elbow. This will cause his arm to bend and simultaneously drop.

Knife/Box Cutter Takeaway #1 Stab (continued)

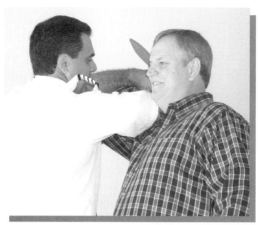

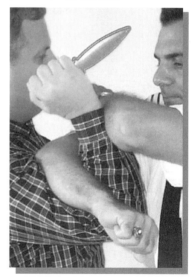

> 5. Step toward the attacker and simultaneously push back with your blocking arm while pulling toward you with your free hand. This will cause pain in the attacker's shoulder and arm. (The attacker will drop the knife.... If he doesn't drop the knife, keep stepping forward until he falls to the ground.)

B. Knife/Box Cutter Takeaway #2 Slice

1. If the attacker is holding the knife in the manner depicted above, he is attempting to cut you with a slicing motion.

Knife/Box Cutter Takeaway #2 Slice (continued)

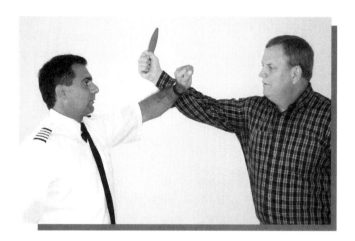

2. Mirror yourself to the attacker and block the knife hand with your forearm.

Knife/Box Cutter Takeaway #2 Slice (continued)

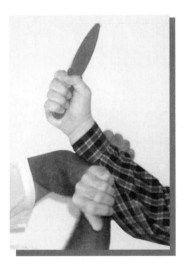

3. With your free hand, come under your blocking hand as shown above.

Knife/Box Cutter Takeaway #2 Slice (continued)

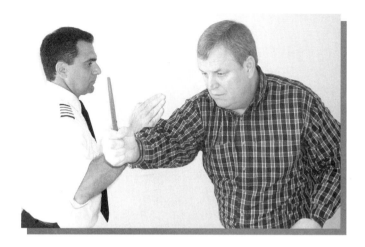

4. Re-direct the attacker's momentum away from you with your free hand.

Knife/Box Cutter Takeaway #2 Slice (continued)

5. Trap the arm of the attacker on your hip.

Knife/Box Cutter Takeaway #2 Slice (continued)

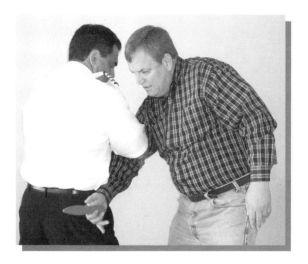

6. Elbow strike the attacker's arm at the bicep muscle. This will cause him to drop the knife.

Knife/Box Cutter Takeaway #2 Slice (continued)

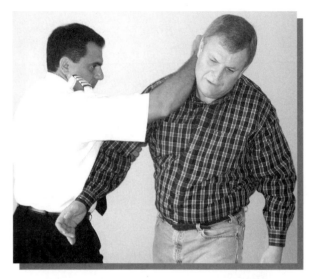

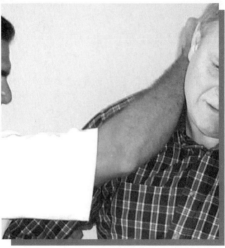

7. Using your forearm, strike the attacker on the side of the neck. This will stun the attacker and cause him to black out.*

C. Knife/Box Cutter Takeaway #3 Thrust

1. If the attacker is attempting to thrust his knife into you as depicted above . . .

Knife/Box Cutter Takeaway #3 Thrust (continued)

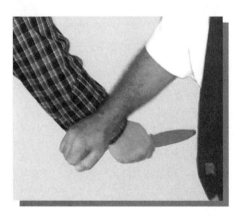

2. Re-direct the blade of the knife as shown . . .

WEAPON TAKEAWAYS

Knife/Box Cutter Takeaway #3 Thrust (continued)

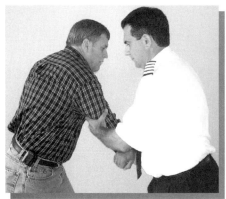

3. Grab the arm of the attacker above the elbow and simultaneously pull him toward you.

4. Follow up with an elbow strike to the throat.

12

COMBINATION MANEUVERS

A. Pilot in Distress #1

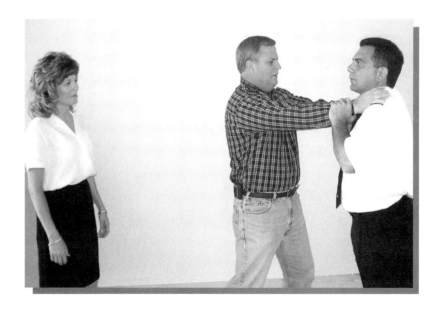

1. In this situation, a pilot is under attack . . .

Pilot in Distress #1 (continued)

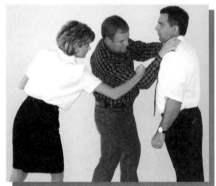

2. A crew member does a hammer fist on the attacker's arm . . .

COMBINATION MANEUVERS

Pilot in Distress #1 (continued)

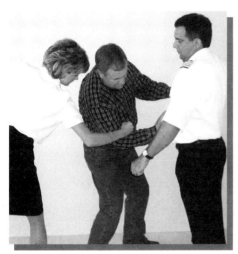

3. Thus causing the attacker to release his grip.

4. The pilot then follows up with a palm heel strike to the face.

B. Pilot in Distress #2

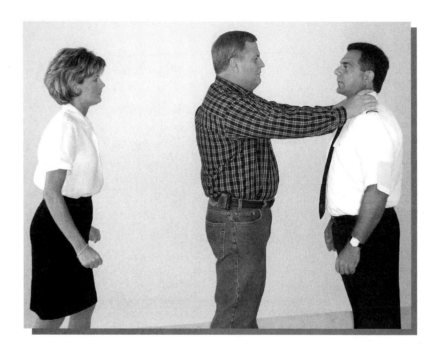

1. In this situation, a pilot is under attack.

Pilot in Distress #2 (continued)

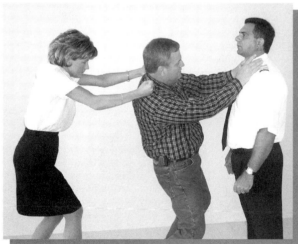

2. A crew member performs a hammer fist on top of the shoulders of the attacker, thus causing him to release his grip. As in the previous situation, the pilot can then follow up with a palm heel strike to the face.

C. Pilot on the Ground #3

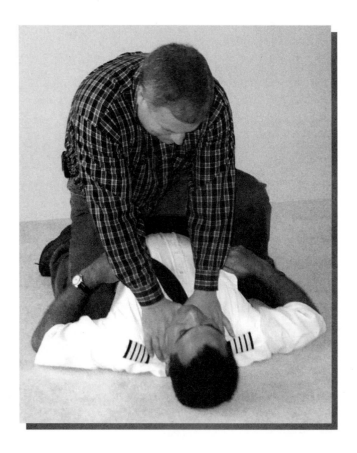

1. The situation above depicts a pilot on the ground being choked by an attacker.

Pilot on the Ground #3 (continued)

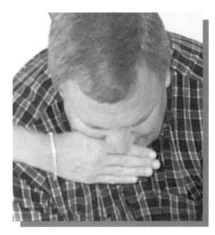

2. A crew member applies pressure under the nose of the attacker, thus causing him to release his grip on the pilot.

Pilot on the Ground #3 (continued)

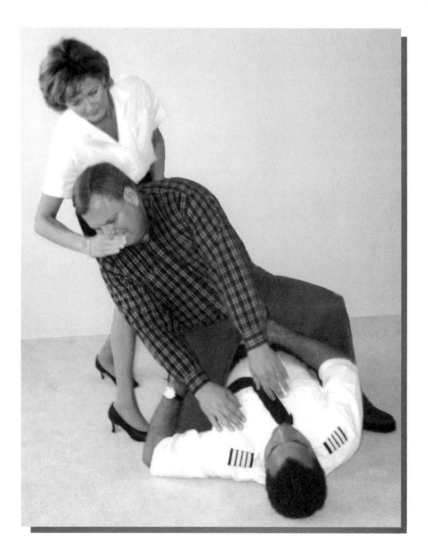

3. The pilot may then follow up with a hammer fist to the groin.

13

THE USE OF COMMONLY FOUND OBJECTS ON AN AIRCRAFT

NOTE: The items listed are not all-inclusive. You must familiarize yourself with all of the objects on your particular aircraft. Should a situation arise, you must use your imagination and creativity to employ all available resources on board in order to distract, disable, or stun an aggressor.

I. Cockpit Items

1. Clothes Hangers
- Striking instrument

2. Crash Axe
- Striking instrument . . . **May cause serious bodily harm or even death**
- Do not throw—If you miss they have a lethal weapon
- Must get close to deliver effective blows

3. Escape Rope
- Can be used as a restraint

4. Eyeglass/Sunglass Ear Piece
- Ear piece can be snapped off and used to poke, jab, or stab
- Must get close to be effective

5. Fire Extinguisher
- Striking instrument
- Blocking instrument
- Spray to the face to distract

6. Flex Cuffs
- Used as a restraint

THE USE OF COMMONLY FOUND OBJECTS ON AN AIRCRAFT

7. Handheld Microphone
- Swing it, using the microphone end as a striking instrument or to keep attackers at bay
- Cord can be used as a restraint

8. Jet Bridge/Cockpit Keys
- Hold the key like you would hold a knife . . . with the key sticking out of the bottom of the fist. With a hammer fist or slicing motion, strike the attacker
- Must get close to be effective

9. Kit Bags
- Blocking instrument

10. Life Vests (Inflated)
- Blocking instrument
- Can be used to ward off blows or a knife attack

11. Log Books
- Striking instrument
- Blocking instrument

12. Maglite Flashlight
- Striking instrument

13. Uniform Belts
- Used as a restraint

14. UNIFORM JACKETS AND OVERCOATS
- Can be thrown over an aggressor to gain control
- Can be used to entangle the hands of an aggressor if armed with a knife

15. UNIFORM TIE (NON-CLIP-ON)
- Used as a restraint

16. WRITING PENS/PENCILS
- Used to poke, jab, and stab
- Must get close to be effective

II. FLIGHT ATTENDANT CARTS AND GALLEY ITEMS

1. **APRONS**
   - Can be used to entangle the hands of an aggressor if armed with a knife

2. **BAGS OF ICE**
   - Blocking device
   - Can be thrown to distract
   - Caution . . . If thrown at an aggressor, it may be returned at you with force

3. **CANNED BEVERAGES AND WATER BOTTLES**
   - Can be thrown to distract
   - Caution . . . If thrown at an aggressor, it may be returned at you with force

4. **CART DRAWERS**
   - Blocking instrument
   - Striking instrument

5. **COFFEEPOTS**
   - Striking instrument

6. **DRINKING GLASSES (FIRST CLASS)**
   - Can be thrown to distract
   - Caution . . . If thrown at an aggressor, it may be returned at you with force

- Can be broken and used as a sharp cutting instrument
- Must get close to be effective

7. **EYEGLASS/SUNGLASS EAR PIECE**

- Ear piece can be snapped off and used to poke, jab, or stab
- Must get close to be effective

8. **GLASS PLATES (FIRST CLASS)**

- Can be thrown to distract
- Caution . . . If thrown at an aggressor, it may be returned at you with force

9. **HOT LIQUID (COFFEE AND WATER)**

- Can be thrown in the face to disable

10. **JET BRIDGE/COCKPIT KEYS**

- Hold the key like you would hold a knife . . . with the key sticking out of the bottom of the fist. With a hammer fist or slicing motion, strike the attacker
- Must get close to be effective

11. **METAL CART TRAYS**

- Blocking instrument
- Striking instrument

12. **PITCHERS**

- Striking instrument
- Contents can be thrown in the face to distract or disable

13. **PLASTIC CUPS**
    - Can be broken and used as a sharp cutting instrument
    - Must get close to be effective

14. **PLASTIC EATING UTENSILS**
    - Used to poke, jab and stab
    - Must get close to be effective

15. **PLASTIC ICE HAMMER**
    - Striking instrument

16. **PLASTIC MEAL TRAYS**
    - Blocking instrument
    - Striking instrument

17. **SERVICE CARTS**
    - Ramming instrument
    - Can also be used to block aisles

18. **UNIFORM BELTS**
    - Used as a restraint

19. **UNIFORM JACKETS AND OVERCOATS**
    - Can be thrown over an aggressor to gain control
    - Can be used to entangle the hands of an aggressor if armed with a knife

20. **UNIFORM TIE (NON-CLIP-ON)**
    - Used as a restraint

21. **WINE AND CHAMPAGNE BOTTLES**
    - Striking instruments

22. WRITING PENS/PENCILS

- Used to poke, jab, and stab
- Must get close to be effective

III. Cabin Items

1. Blankets
- Can be thrown over an aggressor to gain control
- Can be used to entangle the hands of an aggressor if armed with a knife

2. Bullhorn/Megaphone
- Can be used as a noise distracter

3. Clothes Hangers
- Striking instrument

4. Curtains (Galley, Coach, and First Class)
- Can be ripped down and thrown over an aggressor to gain control
- Can be used to entangle the hands of an aggressor if armed with a knife

5. Demo Seat Belt
- Swing it in an arc as a striking instrument or to keep an attacker at bay

6. Fire Extinguishers
- Striking instrument
- Blocking instrument
- Spray to the face to distract

7. **FLASHLIGHTS (FLIGHT ATTENDANT JUMPSEATS)**
   - Striking instrument

8. **LIFE VESTS (INFLATED)**
   - Blocking instrument
   - Can be used to ward off blows or a knife attack

9. **LUGGAGE (OVERHEAD BINS)**
   - Blocking instrument
   - Can be used to block aisles

10. **MAGAZINES**
    - When rolled up, can be used as a striking instrument

11. **MEDICAL KIT**
    - Contains scissors which can be used as a weapon
    - Must get close to be effective

12. **OXYGEN WALK-AROUND BOTTLES**
    - Striking instrument
    - Blocking instrument

13. **PASSENGER OXYGEN MASKS**
    - Can be dropped all at once from the cockpit in order to distract.
    - Cords can be used as a restraint

14. **PILLOWS**
    - Blocking instrument

15. PUBLIC ADDRESS/INTERPHONE HANDSET
- Striking instrument

16. SEAT CUSHIONS
- Blocking instrument
- Can be used to force a passenger to retreat

14

LAW ENFORCEMENT RESPONSE TO A HIJACKING—WHAT TO EXPECT

If the aircraft is on the ground with the hijackers/terrorists on board, have confidence that you will be rescued. Waiting for police response may seem like an eternity. Have patience and maintain your composure. The first forty-five minutes of a hijacking are critical . . . tensions will be extremely high and there will be much confusion. **DO NOT PANIC! BE PATIENT . . . PATIENCE IS CRITICAL!** Crew members must remember that if you panic, the passengers will panic. Everyone must do as he or she is told to keep the situation from escalating. In the early stages of a hijacking, it is best to cooperate. Follow instructions and avoid looking directly at the terrorists/hijackers.

When SWAT Teams board the aircraft and gain control, they will do so by utilizing speed, surprise, and violent action. **STRICTLY OBEY THE COMMANDS OF THE SWAT TEAM.** They will employ methods and procedures to make the aircraft safe.

Since law enforcement personnel do not know who the "bad guys" are, everyone will be treated firmly. Understand that there could be "sleepers" among the crew and passengers who have not yet surfaced. Even a crew member in uniform will be considered suspicious until all of the hijackers/terrorists have been positively identified. It is likely that the terrorists/hijackers may change clothes with passengers or members of the crew. Once crew members have been positively identified, they will be asked to assist in pointing out the hijackers/terrorists and in helping passengers with their needs.

Gather intelligence information about the hijackers/terrorists that could be valuable to law enforcement personnel. Such information might include:
1) Types of weapons used
   (handguns, shotguns, submachine guns, knives, clubs)
2) Number of terrorists
3) Nationality
4) Approximate age
5) Sex
6) Languages spoken
7) Physical description
- Clothing
- Hair color and length
- Scars, marks, or tattoos
- Eye color
- Anything that would distinguish the hijackers/terrorists from others aboard the aircraft, such as walking with a limp, amputee, etc.

*IT IS IMPORTANT TO NOTE THAT COMPLIANCE WITH LAW ENFORCEMENT PERSONNEL IS ABSOLUTELY ESSENTIAL FOR A SUCCESSFUL OUTCOME.